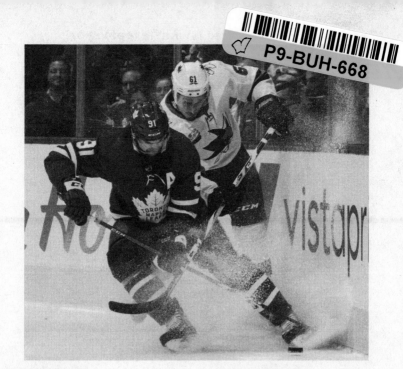

MORE HOCKEY TRIVIA FOR KIDS

Eric Zweig

**illustrations by
Bill Dickson**

Scholastic Canada Ltd.
Toronto New York London Auckland Sydney
Mexico City New Delhi Hong Kong Buenos Aires

To Amanda, whose favourite team sport is still baseball, and to Brent too.
— Eric

Scholastic Canada Ltd.
604 King Street West, Toronto, Ontario M5V 1E1, Canada

Scholastic Inc.
557 Broadway, New York, NY 10012, USA

Scholastic Australia Pty Limited
PO Box 579, Gosford, NSW 2250, Australia

Scholastic New Zealand Limited
Private Bag 94407, Botany, Manukau 2163, New Zealand

Scholastic Children's Books
Euston House, 24 Eversholt Street, London NW1 1DB, UK

Library and Archives Canada Cataloguing in Publication
Title: More hockey trivia for kids / Eric Zweig ; illustrations by Bill Dickson
Other titles: Hockey trivia
Names: Zweig, Eric, 1963- author. | Dickson, Bill, 1949- illustrator.
Identifiers: Canadiana 20190060719 | ISBN 9781443146807 (softcover)
Subjects: LCSH: Hockey—Miscellanea—Juvenile literature. | LCSH: National Hockey League—
Miscellanea—
Juvenile literature.
Classification: LCC GV847.25 .Z947 2019 | DDC j796.962—dc23

Photos ©: cover, title page: Mark Blinch/NHLI/Getty Images; 13: Icon Sportswire/Getty Images;
14: Dave Reginek/NHLI/Getty Images; 33: Andre Ringuette/NHLI/Getty Images; 34: Jonathan
Kozub/NHLI/Getty Images; 38: Juan Ocampo/NHLI/Getty Images; 63: Canada Post © 2016;
65: Canada Post © 2017; 73: Marianna Massey/Getty Images; 96: Icon Sportswire/Getty
Images; 102: Jamie Squire/Getty Images; 111: Dave Sandford/NHLI/Getty Images.

www.scholastic.ca

6 5 4 3 2 1   Printed in Canada 121   19 20 21 22 23

MIX
Paper from
responsible sources
FSC **FSC® C004071**
www.fsc.org

Introduction

This is the fourth of these hockey trivia books I've done, and sometimes I worry that I will run out of stories to tell! The good news is, there's always something happening in hockey to create new ones. For me — who loves the old-time stuff even more than anything that's going on today — the best news is that there are often some interesting old stories that tie into the new ones.

I'll give you an example of what I mean by asking two trivia questions. The first question is: Which team is the only one to win the Stanley Cup at least once during every decade from the 1910s to the 1990s?

The second question is: Which city will be the next to get a new NHL expansion team, starting in the 2021–22 season?

The answers are in this book, but I'm just going to tell you. The first is the Montreal Canadiens. The second is Seattle.

And here's what makes that so interesting to me: If you've read some of my other books, you might know that Seattle used to have a professional hockey team. They didn't play in the NHL but in an old-time league called the Pacific Coast Hockey Association (PCHA), whose champions got to play the NHL champions for the Stanley Cup. As it happens, way back in 1917, the Seattle Metropolitans won the PCHA championship and became the first American team to win the Stanley Cup.

Guess who Seattle beat?

None other than the Montreal Canadiens — a team who'd won their first Stanley Cup just one year before!

I like those sorts of stories, and I hope you find lots you like inside this book too.

Origin Story

The National Hockey League — better known as the NHL — is more than 100 years old. It's recognized around the world as the best league in hockey, but in the NHL's early days, there were other leagues to rival it for the top spot. Until the end of the 1925–26 season, championship teams from the Pacific Coast Hockey Association, the Western Canada Hockey League and the Western Hockey League would play the NHL champions to decide the winner of the Stanley Cup. But by the start of the 1926–27 season, the NHL was the only one from that group of top professional leagues that was still in business. There were other pro leagues, but they were considered minor leagues because the quality of play was not at the same level. Since 1927, only NHL teams have been allowed to compete for the Stanley Cup.

From 1972 to 1979, the NHL had a rival league known as the World Hockey Association (WHA). Despite its name, all the teams were based in Canada and the United States. Teams from the WHA did not play for the Stanley Cup — they had their own, the Avco World Trophy. Unfortunately, most WHA teams struggled financially, and in 1979 the WHA went out of business. But four of its teams joined the NHL: the Edmonton Oilers, the New England Whalers (now the Carolina Hurricanes), the Quebec Nordiques (now the Colorado Avalanche) and the Winnipeg Jets.

Today, the top minor professional league in North America is the American Hockey League (AHL). All of the teams in the AHL serve as farm teams for NHL clubs. It's a place for players who aren't quite ready for the NHL to improve their skills. The AHL was formed in 1936–37. It was created by a merger of the Canadian-American Hockey League, which had begun play in 1926, and the International Hockey League, which started in 1929. Many of the top hockey-playing nations in Europe have their own professional leagues too.

Before players are ready for professional hockey, they play junior hockey. Junior hockey is generally for players between the ages of 16 and 20. In Canada, the top junior leagues are the Ontario Hockey League (OHL), the Western Hockey League (WHL) and the Quebec Major Junior Hockey League (QMJHL). The United States and many European countries also have junior leagues. Even so, most players who make it to the NHL from the United States do it by playing university or college hockey, which is organized by the National Collegiate Athletic Association (NCAA).

The Best of the Best

Who's the greatest player in the NHL? What even defines "greatest player"? Is it leading his team to the Stanley Cup? Or is it individual success, like winning the Art Ross Trophy as the league's leading scorer? It's a debate that's hard to win, but it's one that fans and the media never seem to get tired of.

Three names usually come up when people debate the best player in history: Wayne Gretzky, Bobby Orr and Gordie Howe. Howe passed away in 2016, so he can't offer his opinion anymore, but Gretzky and Orr would tell you that Howe was the best. Howe played in the NHL with the Detroit Red Wings for 25 years, from 1946 to 1971, and won the Stanley Cup four times. After a brief retirement, he played six seasons in the rival

WHA before returning to the NHL in 1979–80. Howe turned 52 years old that season, but he still played all 80 games on the schedule and had 15 goals and 26 assists for 41 points.

When he retired again in 1980, Howe's NHL totals stood at 801 goals and 1,049 assists for 1,850 points in 1,767 games. Nobody thought those records could be broken — and no one has surpassed his record for games played yet — but Wayne Gretzky would shatter his scoring marks. Gretzky set 61 NHL records during his 20 seasons in the league from 1979 to 1999. Most of those records still stand. Hockey was a wide-open game during most of Gretzky's career, with many high-scoring games. But during the late 1990s and into the 2010s, the game shifted to a more defensive style of play, with fewer goals. Gretzky's records seem unbeatable. Recent rule changes — like smaller

goalie pads — have opened up the game again, but it seems unlikely his records will fall any time soon.

Bobby Orr's career was much shorter than Gretzky's or Howe's, but it was pretty spectacular! Orr's offensive skill changed the way defencemen played the game. He was the first defenceman in NHL history to top 100 points in a season — which he did six times! — and he is still the only defenceman ever to lead the league in scoring, which he did twice. Orr played from 1966 to 1978 and was plagued by chronic knee injuries. But even though his career was relatively short, he has many supporters as the greatest player in history.

100 Greatest Players

The NHL turned 100 on December 19, 2017. As part of its birthday celebrations, a panel of distinguished members of the hockey community — including executives, media professionals and NHL alumni — compiled this list of 100 all-time greats:

Sid Abel
(C, 1938–39 to 1953–54)

Syl Apps
(C, 1936–37 to 1947–48)

Andy Bathgate
(C, 1952–53 to 1970–71)

Jean Beliveau
(C, 1950–51 to 1970–71)

Max Bentley
(C, 1940–42 to 1953–54)

Toe Blake
(LW, 1934–35 to 1947–48)

Mike Bossy
(RW, 1977–78 to 1986–87)

Ray Bourque
(D, 1979–80 to 2000–01)

Johnny Bower
(G, 1953–54 to 1969–70)

Turk Broda
(G, 1936–37 to 1951–52)

Martin Brodeur
(G, 1991–92 to 2014–15)

Johnny Bucyk
(LW, 1955–56 to 1977–78)

Pavel Bure
(RW, 1991–92 to 2002–03)

Chris Chelios
(D, 1983–84 to 2009–10)

King Clancy
(D, 1921–22 to 1936–37)

Bobby Clarke
(C, 1969–70 to 1983–84)

Paul Coffey
(D, 1980–81 to 2000–01)

Charlie Conacher
(RW, 1929–30 to 1940–41)

Yvan Cournoyer
(RW, 1963–64 to 1978–79)

Sidney Crosby
(C, 2005–06 to present)

Pavel Datsyuk
(C, 2001–02 to 2015–16)

Alex Delvecchio
(C, 1950–51 to 1973–74)

Marcel Dionne
(C, 1971–72 to 1988–89)

Ken Dryden
(G, 1970–71 to 1978–79)

Bill Durnan
(G, 1943–44 to 1949–50)

Phil Esposito
(C, 1963–64 to 1980–81)

Tony Esposito
(G, 1968–69 to 1983–84)

Sergei Fedorov
(C, 1990–91 to 2008–09)

Peter Forsberg
(C, 1994–95 to 2010–11)

Ron Francis
(C, 1994–95 to 2003–04)

Grant Fuhr
(G, 1981–82 to 1999–2000)

Bob Gainey
(LW, 1973–74 to 1988–89)

Mike Gartner
(RW, 1979–80 to 1997–98)

Bernie Geoffrion
(RW, 1950–51 to 1967–68)

Wayne Gretzky
(C, 1979–80 to 1998–99)

Glenn Hall
(G, 1952–53 to 1970–71)

Doug Harvey
(D, 1947–48 to 1968–69)

Dominik Hasek
(G, 1990–91 to 2007–08)

Tim Horton
(D, 1949–50 to 1973–74)

Gordie Howe
(RW, 1946–47 to 1979–80)

Bobby Hull
(LW, 1957–58 to 1979–80)

Brett Hull
(RW, 1986–87 to 2005–06)

Jaromir Jagr
(RW, 1990–91 to 2017–18)

Patrick Kane
(RW, 2007–08 to present)

Duncan Keith
(D, 2005–06 to present)

Red Kelly
(D, 1947–48 to 1966–67)

Ted Kennedy
(C, 1942–43 to 1956–57)

Dave Keon
(C, 1960–61 to 1981–82)

Jari Kurri
(RW, 1980–81 to 1997–98)

Elmer Lach
(C, 1940–41 to 1953–54)

Guy Lafleur
(RW, 1971–72 to 1990–91)

Pat LaFontaine
(C, 1983–84 to 1997–98)

Brian Leetch
(D, 1987–88 to 2005–06)

Jacques Lemaire
(C, 1967–68 to 1978–79)

Mario Lemieux
(C, 1984–85 to 2005–06)

Eric Lindros
(C, 1992–93 to 2006–07)

Ted Lindsay
(LW, 1944–45 to 1964–65)

Al MacInnis
(D, 1981–82 to 2003–04)

Frank Mahovlich
(LW, 1956–57 to 1973–74)

Mark Messier
(C, 1979–80 to 2003–04)

Stan Mikita
(C, 1958–59 to 1979–80)

Mike Modano
(C, 1988–89 to 2010–11)

Dickie Moore
(LW, 1951–52 to 1967–68)

Howie Morenz
(C, 1923–24 to 1936–37)

Scott Niedermayer
(D, 1991–92 to 2009–10)

Joe Nieuwendyk
(C, 1986–87 to 2006–07)

Adam Oates
(C, 1985–86 to 2003–04)

Bobby Orr
(D, 1966–67 to 1978–79)

Alex Ovechkin
(LW, 2005–06 to present)

Bernie Parent
(G, 1965–66 to 1978–79)

Brad Park
(D, 1968–69 to 1984–85)

Gilbert Perreault
(C, 1970–71 to 1986–87)

Jacques Plante
(G, 1952–53 to 1972–73)

Denis Potvin
(D, 1973–74 to 1987–88)

Chris Pronger
(D, 1993–94 to 2011–12)

Jean Ratelle
(C, 1960–61 to 1980–81)

Henri Richard
(C, 1955–56 to 1974–75)

Maurice Richard
(RW, 1942–43 to 1959–60)

Larry Robinson
(D, 1972–73 to 1991–92)

Luc Robitaille
(LW, 1986–87 to 2005–06)

Patrick Roy
(G, 1984–85 to 2002–03)

Joe Sakic
(C, 1988–89 to 2008–09)

Borje Salming
(D, 1973–74 to 1989–90)

Denis Savard
(C, 1980–81 to 1996–97)

Serge Savard
(D, 1966–67 to 1982–83)

Terry Sawchuk
(G, 1949–50 to 1969–70)

Milt Schmidt
(C, 1936–37 to 1954–55)

Teemu Selanne
(RW, 1992–93 to 2013–14)

Brendan Shanahan
(LW, 1987–88 to 2008–09)

Eddie Shore
(D, 1926–27 to 1939–40)

Darryl Sittler
(C, 1970–71 to 1984–85)

Billy Smith
(G, 1971–72 to 1988–89)

Peter Stastny
(C, 1980–81 to 1994–95)

Scott Stevens
(D, 1982–83 to 2003–04)

Mats Sundin
(C, 1990–91 to 2008–09)

Jonathan Toews
(C, 2007–08 to present)

Bryan Trottier
(C, 1975–76 to 1993–94)

Georges Vezina
(G, 1917–18 to 1925–26)

Steve Yzerman
(C, 1983–84 to 2005–06).

Young Guns

Connor McDavid and Wayne Gretzky are the only players in NHL history to win the Art Ross Trophy as scoring leader more than once before age 22. In all, Gretzky won the Art Ross Trophy a record 10 times in his career.

Season-Starting Streak

Despite the spectacular start to his NHL career, it took Connor McDavid until the fourth game of his fourth season, in 2018–19, to set his first NHL record. McDavid picked up a point on nine straight Edmonton Oilers goals to start the season. The previous record, of seven straight points to start a season, was set by Adam Oates of the Detroit Red Wings in 1986–87.

BY THE NUMBERS

Connor McDavid reached the 100-point mark for the first time in his career in just his second NHL season, 2016–17. He had 30 goals and 70 assists for exactly 100 points, and he won his first scoring title that year too. At just 20 years and 2 months old, McDavid was the sixth-youngest player in NHL history to score 100 points. Here's a look at the top 10:

PLAYER	TEAM	AGE / SEASON
Sidney Crosby	Pittsburgh	18 years, 8 months in 2005–06
Dale Hawerchuk	Winnipeg	18 years, 11 months in 1981–82
Wayne Gretzky	Edmonton	19 years, 2 months in 1979–80
Mario Lemieux	Pittsburgh	19 years, 6 months in 1984–85
Jimmy Carson	Los Angeles	19 years, 8 months in 1987–88
Connor McDavid	Edmonton	20 years, 2 months in 2016–17
Pierre Larouche	Pittsburgh	20 years, 4 months in 1975–76
Alex Ovechkin	Washington	20 years, 6 months in 2005–06
Pierre Turgeon	Buffalo	20 years, 7 months in 1989–90
Rob Brown	Pittsburgh	20 years, 11 months in 1988–89

MASCOT MAYHEM

As of the 2018–19 season, 30 of the 31 NHL teams had their own mascot. The newest addition to the mascot crew is Gritty, of the Philadelphia Flyers. Gritty was unveiled on September 24, 2018, at a Philadelphia children's museum. He's a 2.13 metre (7 ft.) orange monster in a Flyers uniform, with big googlie eyes, long hair and a scraggly playoff beard. Some people thought Gritty looked a little too scary, and even disturbing; however, he quickly became a big hit with Flyers fans. But Gritty is not the Flyers' first mascot. They briefly had one named Slapshot in 1976.

The Toronto Maple Leafs battle the Detroit Red Wings in the 2017 NHL Centennial Classic.

100 Years of History

The 2017–18 hockey season marked 100 years of NHL history. The league actually began celebrating its centennial during the 2016–17 season, starting things off on January 1, 2017, with an outdoor game in Toronto dubbed the NHL Centennial Classic. There were 40,148 fans in attendance at Exhibition Stadium (now BMO Field) to see the Toronto Maple Leafs defeat the Detroit Red Wings 5–4 in overtime.

The Toronto Maple Leafs also celebrated 100 years of their NHL history during the 2017–18 season. The first games in NHL history were played on December 19, 1917. To celebrate, on December 19, 2017, the Leafs played a rare mid-week afternoon game. They asked their season-ticket holders to bring a child to the game with them, or to donate the ticket back to the team, which gave them to school-aged fans. The Leafs beat the Carolina Hurricanes 8–1 that day, a much better result for Toronto fans than in 1917. That night, the Montreal Wanderers defeated the Toronto Arenas 10–9.

Did You Know?

The only NHL team that does not currently have a mascot is the New York Rangers.

Did You Know?

NHL legends Wayne Gretzky and Mark Messier started their pro careers in the WHA.

NAME GAME:
Classic Edition

Even though his career ended in 1925, Georges Vezina is still a famous name in hockey. That's because back in 1926, the Montreal Canadiens donated the Vezina Trophy to honour the best goalie in the NHL each season. Vezina's career in goal began in 1910. He played every game the Canadiens had for 15 years. He was always calm and in control on the ice. People called Vezina "the Chicoutimi Cucumber" because of the old expression "cool as a cucumber" and because of his hometown of Chicoutimi, Quebec.

Going Down in History

When the NHL began, it was against league rules for goalies to drop to the ice to make a save. They had to remain standing on their skates at all times — if they sprawled on the ice, they faced a minor penalty. Goalies were required to serve their own minor penalties until the 1941–42 season, but the rule about falling to the ice didn't last nearly that long. Just three weeks into the first season, on January 9, 1918, it was announced that the rule would be deleted, thus permitting the goalkeeper to adopt "any attitude he pleases in stopping a shot."

Hart to Hart

When Connor McDavid and the Edmonton Oilers faced Taylor Hall and the New Jersey Devils on October 6, 2018, it marked just the second time in NHL history that the previous two winners of the Hart Memorial Trophy faced each other in a season opener. McDavid had won the award for NHL MVP in 2016–17, while Hall had won it in 2017–18.

The first time that happened was the season opener between the Detroit Red Wings and the New York Rangers on October 11, 1950. That game actually featured the previous three winners of the Hart Memorial Trophy, with Chuck Rayner (1949–50) and Buddy O'Connor (1947–48) of the Rangers facing Sid Abel (1948–49) of the Red Wings.

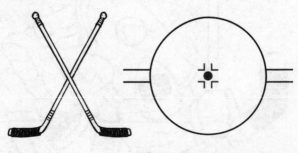

BY THE NUMBERS

Only five players in NHL history have scored 50 goals in a single season before their 21st birthday. Here's a look at that list:

PLAYER	TEAM	AGE / SEASON
Wayne Gretzky	Edmonton	19 years, 2 months in 1979–80
Jimmy Carson	Los Angeles	19 years, 8 months in 1987–88
Steven Stamkos	Tampa Bay	20 years, 2 months in 2009–10
Pierre Larouche	Pittsburgh	20 years, 5 months in 1975–76
Alex Ovechkin	Washington	20 years, 6 months in 2005–06

Hat Trick
Fights Cancer

At the start of training camp before the 2017–18 season, Brian Boyle of the New Jersey Devils was diagnosed with a type of bone-marrow cancer. Boyle worked his way back into the lineup by November 1, 2017, missing only three other games that season. He scored 13 goals in 69 games, including a memorable one on November 24, 2017 — New Jersey's Hockey Fights Cancer night. Hockey Fights Cancer is an annual campaign organized by the NHL and the NHL Players' Association since 1998. Almost a year later, on November 5, 2018, Boyle scored his first career hat trick in the Devils' 5–1 win over the Penguins, which just happened to be the Hockey Fights Cancer night in Pittsburgh.

NAME GAME:
Classic Edition

Gordie Howe was so good for such a long time it just became natural to refer to him as "Mr. Hockey." A few other players had been called by that nickname before Howe, but it described him so perfectly that it's unlikely anyone else will ever be known as "Mr. Hockey."

MR. HOCKEY

The Ice Lions Roar

Kenya, in East Africa, hardly seems like hockey country. Even so, a group of young men there had seen the sport on TV and online and decided it looked like fun. They set up a team called the Kenya Ice Lions, and play on a rink in the capital city of Nairobi. It's the very first rink in East or Central Africa. It only has temporary boards and a small ice surface. The players themselves didn't have full equipment — or a goalie! Instead, they practised with a large rubber penguin in net. If the puck hit the penguin, it counted as a goal. Since they were the only team in Kenya, the Ice Lions never played a real game. That all changed in the summer of 2018.

The Ice Lions were discovered when they filmed some of their practices in Nairobi and posted the videos to YouTube. Tim Hortons invited them to play against a team of firefighters in Toronto. The Kenyan team were gifted full gear, including official team uniforms. But the best part was when NHL stars Sidney Crosby and Nathan MacKinnon showed up to play with them!

Arnold Mburu told a Toronto newspaper: "I had no idea, we were all dressed up and because we were a few guys short, they told us they are going to get extra guys. But then Crosby walks in. And MacKinnon's face is right behind him. And I can't believe it."

The Ice Lions roared in the friendly exhibition game, winning it 5 to 4. Then again, they have had lots of practice playing with a Penguin!

BY THE NUMBERS

Most points in a single NHL game:

PLAYER	TEAM	POINTS
Darryl Sittler	Toronto Maple Leafs	10
Maurice Richard	Montreal Canadiens	8
Bert Olmstead	Montreal Canadiens	8
Tom Bladon	Philadelphia Flyers	8
Bryan Trottier	New York Islanders	8
Peter Stastny	Quebec Nordiques	8
Anton Stastny	Quebec Nordiques	8
Wayne Gretzky	Edmonton Oilers	8
Wayne Gretzky	Edmonton Oilers	8
Paul Coffey	Edmonton Oilers	8
Patrik Sundstrom	Washington Capitals	8
Mario Lemieux	Pittsburgh Penguins	8
Bernie Nicholls	Los Angeles Kings	8
Mario Lemieux	Pittsburgh Penguins	8
Mario Lemieux	Pittsburgh Penguins	8
Sam Gagner	Edmonton Oilers	8

GOALS/ASSISTS	DATE
6G 4A	February 7, 1976
5G 3A	December 28, 1944
4G 4A	January 9, 1954
4G 4A	December 11, 1977
5G 3A	December 23, 1978
4G 4A	February 22, 1981
3G 5A	February 22, 1981
3G 5A	November 19, 1983
4G 4A	January 4, 1984
2G 6A	March 14, 1986
3G 5A	April 22, 1988°
2G 6A	October 15, 1988
2G 6A	December 1, 1988
5G 3A	December 31, 1988
5G 3A	April 25, 1989°
4G 4A	February 2, 2012

° accomplished in a playoff game

Trophy Tales

Stanley Cup wins for each NHL franchise in the Eastern Conference, Atlantic Division:

Boston Bruins
First season: 1924–25
Stanley Cup wins: 6
Years: 1928–29; 1938–39; 1940–41;
1969–70; 1971–72; 2010–11

Buffalo Sabres
First season: 1970–71
Stanley Cup wins: 0

Detroit Red Wings
First season: 1926–27
(Detroit Cougars through 1929–30;
Detroit Falcons through 1931–32)
Stanley Cup wins: 11
Years: 1935–36; 1936–37; 1942–43; 1949–50;
1951–52; 1953–54; 1954–55; 1996–97;
1997–98; 2001–02; 2007–08

Florida Panthers
First season: 1993–94
Stanley Cup wins: 0

Montreal Canadiens
First season: 1909–10
   (First NHL season: 1917–18)
Stanley Cup wins: 24
Years: 1915–16; 1923–24; 1929–30; 1930–31;
      1943–44; 1945–46; 1952–53; 1955–56;
      1956–57; 1957–58; 1958–59; 1959–60;
      1964–65; 1965–66; 1967–68; 1968–69;
      1970–71; 1972–73; 1975–76; 1976–77;
      1977–78; 1978–79; 1985–86; 1992–93

Ottawa Senators
First season: 1992–93
Stanley Cup wins: 0

Tampa Bay Lightning
First season: 1992–93
Stanley Cup wins: 1
Year: 2003–04

Toronto Maple Leafs
First season: 1917–18
   (Toronto Arenas through 1918–19;
   Toronto St. Patricks through 1926–27)
Stanley Cup wins: 13
Years: 1917–18; 1921–22; 1931–32; 1941–42;
      1944–45; 1946–47; 1947–48; 1948–49;
      1950–51; 1961–62; 1962–63; 1963–64;
      1966–67

MASCOT MAYHEM

Harvey the Hound is the mascot of the Calgary Flames, acquired in 1983 as the team's "first pound draft pick." He was the first permanent mascot in NHL history, making his debut on February 16, 1984, in a game against the Pittsburgh Penguins. That night two Calgary players — Lanny McDonald and Doug Risebrough — scored hat tricks in a 10–3 win over Pittsburgh, and Harvey has been popular ever since.

On January 20, 2003, the 1.98 metre (6 ft., 6 in.) dog was taunting the rival team behind the Edmonton bench when Oilers coach Craig MacTavish reached up and ripped out Harvey's red fabric tongue. The incident drew a lot of attention, and at the 2003 NHL All-Star Game a few weeks later, many other team mascots appeared with their own fabric tongues hanging out of their mouths.

Did You Know?

John Tavares holds the record for the most goals scored in the history of the OHL. Between 2005–06 and 2008–09, Tavares scored 215 goals in 247 games over four seasons with the Oshawa Generals and the London Knights.

21st-Century Scorer

On October 7, 2018, Andrei Svechnikov of the Carolina Hurricanes became the first player born in the 21st century to score a goal in the NHL. His goal broke a 5–5 tie and led Carolina to an 8–5 win over the New York Rangers. Svechnikov, who was the second player selected in the 2018 NHL Entry Draft, was born on March 26, 2000.

NAME GAME:
Classic Edition

The Richard brothers are legendary. Maurice was the heart and soul of the Montreal Canadiens during his career with the team from 1942 to 1960. He was known as "the Comet" early in his career, but then one day teammate Ray Getliffe described a play Maurice had made, saying it "went in like a rocket." Sportswriters picked up on that, and soon Maurice was "the Rocket."

Henri Richard was 15 years younger than his famous brother, and when he joined him on the Canadiens as a 19-year-old rookie in 1955, Henri became known as "the Pocket Rocket." Claude was *another* hockey-playing Richard brother, one year younger than Henri. He was sometimes called "the Vest Pocket Rocket." Claude had tryouts with the Canadiens in 1958 and 1959, but he never made it to the NHL.

Sidney's Sis

Taylor Crosby started hanging out at the local rink in Cole Harbour, Nova Scotia, when she was only two weeks old. Her brother, Sidney, was 10 years old then and already attracting national attention. When Taylor began playing hockey, she decided she wanted to be a goalie like her father, Troy, who'd been good enough as a junior to be drafted by the Montreal Canadiens.

Like her brother, Taylor Crosby left Cole Harbour to combine high school with hockey at Shattuck-St. Mary's in Faribault, Minnesota. In four years at Shattuck, she helped the team reach the national tournament four times — and finish as runner-up in her final season, 2013–14. Taylor went on to play university hockey at Minnesota's St. Cloud State. Taylor is now a Pittsburgh Penguin too — sort of. Since graduating in 2018, she's worked for their marketing department.

BY THE NUMBERS

When Auston Matthews of the Toronto Maple Leafs scored four goals in his rookie debut in 2016, it marked the most goals by a player in his first NHL game since December 19, 1917, the very first night of the NHL. Here are the players with three or more goals in their NHL debut:

PLAYER	TEAM	GOALS
Joe Malone	Montreal Canadiens	5
Harry Hyland	Montreal Wanderers	5
Reg Noble	Toronto Arenas	4
Auston Matthews	Toronto Maple Leafs	4
Cy Denneny	Ottawa Senators	3
Alex Smart	Montreal Canadiens	3
Real Cloutier	Quebec Nordiques	3
Fabian Brunnstrom	Dallas Stars	3
Derek Stepan	New York Rangers	3
Ryan Poehling	Montreal Canadiens	3*

Auston Matthews and the four pucks used to score his first career NHL goals.

DATE	FINAL SCORE
December 19, 1917	Montreal 7 at Ottawa 4
December 19, 1917	Toronto 9 at Montreal 10
December 19, 1917	Toronto 9 at Montreal 10
October 12, 2016	Toronto 4 at Ottawa 5
December 19, 1917	Montreal 7 at Ottawa 4
January 14, 1943	Chicago 1 at Montreal 5
October 10, 1979	Atlanta 5 at Quebec 3
October 15, 2008	Nashville 4 at Dallas 6
October 9, 2010	New York 6 at Buffalo 3
April 6, 2019	Toronto 5 at Montreal 6

* also scored the game-winning goal in a shootout

Young Guns

The Winnipeg Jets made Patrik Laine the second pick in the 2016 NHL Entry Draft right after Toronto took Auston Matthews first overall. Both players immediately made it to the NHL. Laine scored 36 goals as an 18-year-old rookie in 2016–17 and had 44 goals in 2017–18, when he was 19. Late in that season, just before he turned 20, Laine set a new NHL record for teens by collecting a point in 15 straight games.

Patrik Laine celebrates a goal in the October 19, 2016, win against the Leafs, where he had a hat trick.

During his streak, Laine scored 18 goals and had 8 assists for 26 points. Before Laine had points in 15 straight, the longest scoring streak by a teenager was 13 games, set in 2014 by Nathan MacKinnon of the Colorado Avalanche when he was an 18-year-old rookie.

BY THE NUMBERS

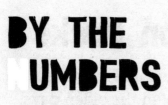

Most NHL goals by a teenager:

PLAYER	TEAM	GOALS	YEARS
Jimmy Carson	Los Angeles Kings	92	1986–1988
Dale Hawerchuk	Winnipeg Jets	85	1981–1983
Patrik Laine	Winnipeg Jets	80	2016–2018
Wayne Gretzky	Edmonton Oilers	76	1979–1981
Brian Bellows	Minnesota North Stars	76	1982–1984

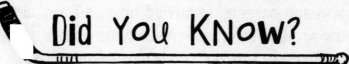

Did You Know?

The youngest player ever to score a goal in the NHL was the Boston Bruins' Bep Guidolin. He was just 16 years and 350 days old when he scored against the Chicago Black Hawks on November 24, 1942. Guidolin got a chance to play in the NHL at 16 because many veteran players had enlisted in the armed forces during World War II.

The Poop on Pucks

What do poop and LED technology have in common? Hockey pucks! In the olden days, frozen horse poop was often used as pucks in outdoor games of shinny. Fast forward to 1994, when the Fox Sports network started broadcasting NHL games in the United States. American viewers complained that they had a hard time following the puck on television. Fox wanted to make sure viewers could always see the fast-moving puck, so the network used infrared technology to follow LED lights that were embedded inside the puck. On a television screen, it showed up as a hazy blue glow around the puck, and whenever the puck travelled 113 km/h (70 mph) or faster, a red comet tail would appear.

The "FoxTrax" system was used for two seasons, from 1996 to 1998, and it was widely mocked by hockey fans. But now the NHL has come up with something new. During the 2019 All-Star Game, the league debuted a system using microchips placed inside the puck and in each player's shoulder pads. This new tech tracks how fast the puck is shot and how fast a player is skating. It can also track where everyone is on the ice at all times and how far each player skates during a game. When the new system goes league-wide during the 2019–20 season, the NHL is betting that the new statistics will attract a lot of interest. Bonus: the new pucks don't smell!

NAME GAME:
Team Names

The Vegas Golden Knights officially became the NHL's 31st franchise on March 1, 2017, playing their first regular-season game on October 6, 2017. The team decided to go with Vegas instead of Las Vegas — the city's full name — because that's what most locals call it. Team owner Bill Foley is a graduate of the U.S. Military Academy, also known as West Point. Its sports teams are known as the Army Black Knights. Foley hoped to use that name too, but he couldn't get permission and went with Golden Knights instead. It's a glitzy name for a glitzy city.

Malcolm Subban stopped 30 shots to help the Vegas Golden Knights beat the Los Angeles Kings 4–1 on December 28, 2018.

MASCOT MAYHEM

Chance is the mascot for the Vegas Golden Knights. It's a fitting name for a team in a city best known for gambling! Chance is a Gila — pronounced "HEE-la" — monster, which is not really a monster at all, but a reclusive lizard native to the southwestern United States. Chance made his debut on October 13, 2017, one week into the Golden Knights' first season.

Fast Forward

The NHL announced on December 4, 2018, that Seattle will become the home of its newest team. The new Seattle team will officially start playing as the NHL's 32nd franchise during the 2021–22 season. The cost of becoming the NHL's newest team is $650 million, which is $150 million more than the $500 million expansion fee paid by the Vegas Golden Knights when they entered the NHL. In 1967, the fee for an NHL expansion team was $2 million.

Pass the Puck, Mate!

Nathan Walker grew up in Sydney, Australia. At the time, hockey wasn't big there, but after watching his older brother play — and seeing the movie *The Mighty Ducks* — Nathan was determined to hit the ice. He became the first Australian to play in the NHL when he was selected by the Washington Capitals in the third round (89th overall) of the 2014 NHL Entry Draft.

Walker debuted with the Capitals on October 7, 2017, scoring a goal in his first game. Walker played only seven games for Washington in 2017–18, spending most of the season in the minors. But Walker was in the lineup for a playoff game with the Capitals during the Capitals' winning run to the Stanley Cup that year, and he became the first Australian to have a playoff point, an assist in their 2–1 win over the Pittsburgh Penguins on May 7, 2018.

Hockey Down Under

The history of hockey in Australia dates back farther than you may think! The first hockey game in Australia took place on October 4, 1904. Two teams adapted a game known as roller polo to the ice of the country's first indoor rink, which had opened the month before. Newspapers advertised it as a polo match before the game, but called it a hockey match the next day. By 1909, there was an annual national tournament, and today there are national amateur leagues for both men and women.

NAME GAME:
Classic Edition

During his heyday with the Chicago Black Hawks in the 1960s, there was no player more exciting than Bobby Hull. He was the fastest skater in the game, and he had the hardest slapshot too. With all that power, combined with his blond good looks, Hull was known as "the Golden Jet." When his son Brett Hull became a huge star in the 1990s, people called *him* "the Golden Brett."

Did You Know?

The top speed of a Zamboni machine is 15.6 km/h (9.7 mph), according to tests done by *Road & Track* magazine in 2005.

MASCOT MAYHEM

Youppi! is the mascot of the Montreal Canadiens. He is big and orange and furry. His name is French for "Yippee!" or "Hooray!" It's officially spelled with an exclamation mark, which he wears on the back of his sweater instead of a number. Youppi! began life as the mascot of baseball's Montreal Expos in 1979. When the Expos left Montreal to become the Washington Nationals after the 2004 season, the Canadiens adopted him as their mascot.

Youppi! was the first mascot ever to be kicked out of a Major League Baseball game. In the 11th inning of a game on August 23, 1989, he took a running leap onto the top of the visitors' dugout. Los Angeles Dodgers manager Tommy Lasorda complained to the umpires about the noise, and Youppi! was ejected! He was later allowed to return to the game as long as he stayed on the Expos' dugout.

Trophy Tales

When Lord Stanley donated his famous cup in 1892, hockey was still an amateur sport — the athletes did not get paid. But in 1906, the defending Stanley Cup champion Montreal Wanderers announced that they were going to start paying some of their players, and professional hockey was born. The Stanley Cup would be the prize.

What would amateur teams do? Thankfully, in February of 1909, a new amateur hockey trophy was donated by Sir H. Montagu Allan, a wealthy businessman from Montreal. The Allan Cup became an important national trophy.

From 1938 until 1971, there were only two Canadian NHL teams. Communities across the country rooted for their home teams and there was strong support for amateur leagues. Today, teams from all over Canada (and occasionally from the United States) still compete for the Allan Cup.

Did You Know?

In the early days of hockey in Canada, the game was played on natural ice. It took cold temperatures to freeze the water into ice, whether it was outside on a lake or river or inside an arena. Canada's first artificial-ice rinks were built in 1911, in Vancouver and Victoria, British Columbia. Artificial-ice rinks have pipes running beneath the floor that can turn water into ice even when it's warm outside.

°C
- 40
- 30
- 20
- 10
- 0
- -10
- -20
- -30

Europe or Bust!

The NHL has begun scheduling more and more games for 1 p.m. eastern time on Saturdays and Sundays. Why? So they can be broadcast on prime time television in Europe! With so many stars from Europe, North American hockey has become very popular there.

Would the NHL ever place an expansion team in a European country? The league hasn't committed to anything, but in 2018, NHL commissioner Gary Bettman said, "If we are going to have a presence in Europe, it would have to be more than one team. The logistics would require a division for it to work." Which is different from him saying "no"!

Olympic Old-Timer

Riikka Sallinen is considered to be Europe's greatest women's hockey player. She represented her native Finland at the first four Women's World Championships and two Winter Olympic Games between 1990 and 2002. Sallinen was the leading scorer, with 12 points (7 goals and 5 assists in 6 games), when women's hockey made its Olympic debut in Nagano, Japan, in 1998. She led Finland to a bronze medal. In 2010, Sallinen was the fourth woman elected to the International Ice Hockey Federation Hall of Fame, following Canada's Angela James and Geraldine Heaney and Cammi Granato of the United States.

After 10 years of retirement, from 2003 until 2013, Sallinen announced she was making a comeback. She returned to the Winter Olympics in 2014 and was back *again* in 2018 to win another bronze medal — at the age of 44.

Playoff Jackpot

In their first season of 2017–18, the Vegas Golden Knights became the most successful expansion team in NHL history — and maybe in all of sports history! The Golden Knights won eight of their first nine games. Hockey experts kept expecting the team to fade . . . but they didn't. Vegas went all the way to the Stanley Cup Final in 2018, becoming the third team in NHL history to play for the Cup in their first season.

The other teams to reach the Final in their first season — the Toronto Arenas in 1918, and the St. Louis Blues in 1968 — faced totally different circumstances. The 1917–18 NHL season was the first official one, so technically all the teams were new! The St. Louis Blues were formed for the 1967–68 season, when the NHL doubled in size from the "Original Six" teams to twelve. To guarantee interest in the new cities, the playoffs were set up that season (and for the next two seasons as well) so that one of the expansion teams would meet one of the established teams for the Cup. The St. Louis Blues reached the Final but were swept by the Canadiens in four straight games.

The Golden Knights had another strong season in 2018–19. They made the playoffs with ease, but their luck ran out in the first round when they lost to the San Jose Sharks.

Ring Tone

In 2018, when the Washington Capitals finally won their first Stanley Cup after 44 seasons, the team celebrated — with bling! In addition to providing commemorative rings for all the players, approximately 500 full-time Capitals employees got one too (although they weren't quite as fancy as the ones for the players).

The tradition of teams presenting special rings to their Stanley Cup winning players didn't really get started until the 1940s and '50s. Before then, players were more likely to receive watches, cufflinks, medallions or coins as a Stanley Cup keepsake. In 1971, the Montreal Canadiens gave each of their players a new television!

Trophy Tales

Stanley Cup wins for each NHL franchise in the Eastern Conference, Metropolitan Division:

Carolina Hurricanes
First season: 1979–80
   (Hartford Whalers through 1996–97)
Stanley Cup wins: 1
Year: 2005–06

Columbus Blue Jackets
First season: 2000–01
Stanley Cup wins: 0

New Jersey Devils
First season: 1974–75
   (Kansas City Scouts through 1975–76;
   Colorado Rockies through 1981–82)
Stanley Cup wins: 3
Years: 1994–95; 1999–2000; 2002–03

New York Islanders
First season: 1972–73
Stanley Cup wins: 4
Years: 1979–80; 1980–81; 1981–82; 1982–83

New York Rangers
First season: 1926–27
Stanley Cup wins: 4
Years: 1927–28; 1932–33; 1939–40; 1993–94

Philadelphia Flyers
First season: 1967–68
Stanley Cup wins: 2
Year: 1973–74; 1974–75

Pittsburgh Penguins
First season: 1967–68
Stanley Cup wins: 5
Years: 1990–91; 1991–92; 2008–09; 2015–16;
2016–17

Washington Capitals
First season: 1974–75
Stanley Cup wins: 1
Year: 2017–18

Hot Dogger!

Phil Kessel of the Pittsburgh Penguins is a speedy player with a knack for putting the puck in the net. One of his nicknames is "Phil the Thrill." But Kessel loves hot dogs almost as much as he loves hockey! When Pittsburgh won the Stanley Cup in 2017, Kessel loaded up the bowl with hot dogs and ate them. The Upper Deck card company issued a series of hockey cards that included pictures of Kessel with the Stanley Cup . . . and his beloved hot dogs.

MASCOT MAYHEM

Mick E. Moose has been the mascot of the Winnipeg Jets since the team moved to the Manitoba capital from Atlanta for the 2011–12 season. Mick works overtime — he is also the mascot of the AHL's Manitoba Moose. Mick made his debut with the Minnesota Moose of the old International Hockey League in 1994 and moved with the team to Winnipeg in 1996.

But Mick was not the first Mascot for the Jets. Benny — who is blue and has a mohawk hairstyle and earmuffs — was the mascot of the original Winnipeg Jets, named in honour of both former Jets owner Ben Hatskin and the Elton John song "Bennie and the Jets." When the franchise moved to Phoenix in 1996, Benny was dropped . . . until the 2016 Heritage Classic outdoor game in Winnipeg, where he staged a comeback. He has re-emerged as a secondary mascot for the current Jets franchise, sometimes appearing along with Mick E. Moose.

Hockey Night in Iowa?

Hockey historians have long argued about where the first "real" hockey game happened. Was it in Montreal? In Halifax? Or maybe Kingston? While the true roots of the game may reach back to England, it's generally recognized that the beginnings of modern hockey in Canada can be traced to a game in Montreal on March 3, 1875.

The first recorded game in the United States was almost 10 years later. On January 12, 1884, the town of Le Mars, Iowa, hosted a team from the village of Seney. Fans paid a dime to watch the game at the new ice rink — and each player had to pay *15* cents just to play!

League of Leagues

The Canadian Hockey League — CHL for short — isn't an actual hockey league. It's an organization that oversees the three major junior hockey leagues in Canada: the Ontario Hockey League (OHL), the Quebec Major Junior Hockey League (QMJHL) and the Western Hockey League (WHL).

And don't let the "C" in the name fool you! All three leagues that make up the CHL have had teams based in the United States. The first American junior team in a Canadian league was the Portland Winterhawks of Portland, Oregon. They joined the WHL for the 1976–77 season.

The first American team in the OHL was the Detroit Compuware Ambassadors, which joined in 1990–91. Over the years, the team has been known as the Detroit Junior Red Wings (1992 to 1995), the Detroit Whalers (1995 to 1997), the Plymouth Whalers (1997 to 2015) and finally the Flint Firebirds (2015 to present).

The Plattsburgh Pioneers from the town of Plattsburgh, New York, were the first American team to join the QMJHL. Their first season was 1984–85. It was their last season, too. In fact, they didn't even last two months! Plattsburgh played only 17 games before the team folded. The QMJHL later added another American team — the Lewiston MAINEiacs — for the 2003–04 season, but they folded eight seasons later, leaving "the Q" 100 percent Canadian. For now.

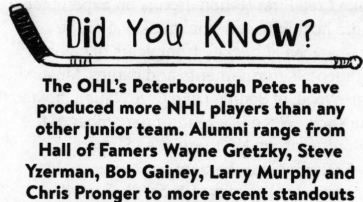

Did You Know?

The OHL's Peterborough Petes have produced more NHL players than any other junior team. Alumni range from Hall of Famers Wayne Gretzky, Steve Yzerman, Bob Gainey, Larry Murphy and Chris Pronger to more recent standouts like Eric Staal, Jordan Staal and Nick Ritchie.

Plains Cree Play-by-Play

On March 24, 2019, Rogers Sportsnet and APTN — the Aboriginal Peoples Television Network — aired the first national television broadcast of an NHL game in the Plains Cree language. The game, between the Montreal Canadiens and the Carolina Hurricanes, was part of the Rogers Hometown Hockey program.

Handling the play-by-play that night was Clarence Iron, who was raised in the Canoe Lake Cree First Nation. Iron is an experienced radio host and well-known as one of the Cree voices of hockey from years of calling Indigenous tournaments and games. Musician Earl Wood, of Saddle Lake Cree Nation, hosted the show. Wood is a founding member of the award-winning Northern Cree Singers.

Rounding out the panel as game analyst was former NHL player John Chabot, who hails from Kitigan Zibi Anishinabeg First Nation. Chabot played eight seasons — and over 500 games! — in the NHL during the 1980s. Chabot helped form the NHL Indigenous Alumni Tour, which travels the country playing games in support of Indigenous youth programs. He also worked as APTN's studio analyst for the 2010 Vancouver Winter Olympic Games and as a coach on APTN's hockey series, *Hit the Ice*. Cree teacher Jason Chamakese, from the Pelican Lake First Nation, translated Chabot's analysis from English to Cree.

Did You Know?

CBC North broadcasters Charlie Panigoniak and Annie Ford called a game between the Ottawa Senators and Montreal Canadiens in Inuktitut as part of Hockey Day in Canada on January 30, 2010. Just a couple of weeks later, at the 2010 Vancouver Winter Olympics, all of Team Canada's hockey games were broadcast in Mi'kmaq, Cree, Dene and Inuktitut.

We Won . . . Finally!

What may just be the longest winless streak in Canadian junior hockey history finally came to an end on January 21, 2018. That Sunday night, the Campbellford Rebels won their first game in almost two years. On January 23, 2016, Campbellford beat the Napanee Raiders 4–3 in overtime. Over the next 77 games, the Rebels suffered 76 losses and 1 tie before finally getting another win with their 9–5 victory over the Gananoque Islanders. "There were 16 players on the noisiest bus I have been on in a long time," said Rebels owner and general manager Michelle Cross after the ride home. "Everyone was smiling ear to ear."

Stay in School

Junior hockey players in Canada are expected to keep up with their homework. The three major junior leagues even provide scholarships to players who want to attend university rather than pursue a pro hockey career. It's not as common as it used to be for players to reach the NHL without even finishing high school, but it does still happen sometimes.

Steve Begin had a solid career, playing 524 games in the NHL over 14 seasons between 1997 and 2013, then started his own engineering company after retiring from the league. But Begin didn't finish high school — until he was challenged to do so by a friend, fellow Quebecer and UFC champion Georges St-Pierre. Begin studied online using an app, hitting the books early in the morning and late at night. He finally got his high-school diploma at the age of 40 in 2018, during a ceremony at the Bell Centre in Montreal.

MASCOT MAYHEM

Fin is the mascot of the Vancouver Canucks. He is a 1.90 metre (6 ft., 3 in.) orca, or killer whale. Fin can spray mist out of his blowhole and often chomps on the heads of unsuspecting fans in the arena. He's also featured in a series of cartoon shorts that play on the scoreboard during Canucks games.

NAME GAME:
Modern Edition

Jonathan Toews was named captain of the Blackhawks in 2008–09, after just one season in the NHL. Toews was only 20 years old, but he was already a true team leader. People call him "Captain Serious."

NAME GAME:
Classic Edition

Wayne Gretzky shattered so many records in his NHL career that people began referring to him as "the Great One." But his teammates didn't usually call him that. To them, he was simply "Gretz."

Mark Messier, who played with Gretzky on the Oilers in the 1980s, was often called "Moose" because he was big and strong. When Messier helped lead the New York Rangers to the Stanley Cup in 1994 after a 54-year championship drought, some people called him "Messiah." But to his teammates, he was mainly known as "Mess."

Mark Messier was included in Canada Post's Great Canadian Forwards stamp collection in 2016. The other players in the lineup were Sidney Crosby, Phil Esposito, Guy Lafleur, Darryl Sittler and Steve Yzerman.

BY THE NUMBERS

Of the top 20 scoring seasons in NHL history, 16 occurred during the 1980s when offensive hockey was at a peak. Here's a look at the top 10 scoring seasons:

PLAYER	TEAM
Wayne Gretzky	Edmonton Oilers
Wayne Gretzky	Edmonton Oilers
Wayne Gretzky	Edmonton Oilers
Wayne Gretzky	Edmonton Oilers
Mario Lemieux	Pittsburgh Penguins
Wayne Gretzky	Edmonton Oilers
Wayne Gretzky	Edmonton Oilers
Mario Lemieux	Pittsburgh Penguins
Wayne Gretzky	Los Angeles Kings
Wayne Gretzky	Edmonton Oilers

*Wayne Gretzky was part of
the Canadian Hockey Legends
stamp collection, released
in 2017. The other players
featured were Maurice Richard,
Jean Beliveau, Gordie Howe,
Bobby Orr and Mario Lemieux.*

POINTS (GOALS, ASSISTS)	SEASON
215 points (52G, 163A)	1985–86
212 points (92G, 120A)	1981–82
208 points (73G, 135A)	1984–85
205 points (87G, 118A)	1983–84
199 points (85G, 114A)	1988–89
196 points (71G, 125A)	1982–83
183 points (62G, 121A)	1986–87
168 points (70G, 98A)	1987–88
168 points (54G, 114A)	1988–89
164 points (55G, 109A)	1980–81

BY THE NUMBERS

New NHL teams and an emphasis on defensive hockey saw a scoring decline in the 1990s and 2000s. But offensive hockey seemed to make a comeback in 2018–19. Here are the top 10 scoring seasons in the NHL since the year 2000:

PLAYER	TEAM
Nikita Kucherov	Tampa Bay Lightning
Joe Thornton	San Jose Sharks
Jaromir Jagr	New York Rangers
Jaromir Jagr	Pittsburgh Penguins
Sidney Crosby	Pittsburgh Penguins
Joe Sakic	Colorado Avalanche
Connor McDavid	Edmonton Oilers
Joe Thornton	San Jose Sharks
Evgeni Malkin	Pittsburgh Penguins
Alex Ovechkin	Washington Capitals

POINTS (GOALS, ASSISTS)	SEASON
128 points (41G, 87A)	2018–19
125 points (29G, 96A)	2005–06
123 points (54G, 69A)	2005–06
121 points (52G, 69A)	2000–01
120 points (36G, 84A)	2006–07
118 points (54G, 64A)	2000–01
116 points (41G, 75A)	2018–19
114 points (22G, 92A)	2006–07
113 points (35G, 78A)	2008–09
112 points (65G, 47A)	2007–08

Million-Dollar Goals

In over 100 years of NHL history, a player has scored five or more goals in a single game 61 times — and only three times since the year 2000. The most recent was on November 24, 2018. Patrik Laine scored five goals for the Winnipeg Jets in an 8–4 win over the St. Louis Blues. Laine's big game did more than just move him to the top of that night's goal-scoring list. It was worth $1 million to one lucky Winnipeg fan!

The man had played a local grocery store's "Score and Win" game, which promised the big cash prize to one lucky winner if a player on the Jets, Flames, Oilers or Canucks scored five goals in a single game. The prize will be paid out at $50,000 per year for 20 years. That's a lot of groceries!

Odds-On Justin

Being one of the 200 or so players chosen in the NHL Entry Draft is an achievement, but it is no guarantee of success. A study of the 2600 players drafted in the 1990s showed that only 19% went on to play in more than 200 NHL games. For first-round picks, that percentage was a solid 63%, but less than 25% of second-rounders reached that mark. By the third round and later, the number had dropped to only 12%.

So when defenseman Justin Braun was selected by the San Jose Sharks in the seventh round of the draft, as the 201st of 211 picks, the odds of him making the NHL were small. Braun played three more years of university hockey before beginning his pro career with the Worcester Sharks of the AHL. He played his first NHL game on November 26, 2010 and finally made it on to the Sharks regular roster in January of 2013. Is he a superstar? Maybe not. But like every player who has achieved success in the NHL, he can claim to be one of the very best hockey players on the planet — an amazing accomplishment!

Mighty Morphin' Leagues

Women and girls have likely been playing hockey in Canada as long as men have. There were popular leagues for women to play in from the late 1910s through the 1930s, but it's never been easy for women to make a living playing hockey.

Several different women's leagues in the 1990s and early 2000s eventually led to the creation of the Canadian Women's Hockey League (CWHL) in 2007–08. Originally based in eastern Canada, the CWHL merged with the Western Women's Hockey League in 2011–12, giving it teams all across the country. Over the years, the CWHL also included teams based in the United States and even China. With its expansion to China in 2017–18, the CWHL announced that it would pay its players for the very first time. Unlike NHL players, who can earn millions of dollars, salaries in the CWHL ranged from only $2,000 to $10,000 per season.

Another women's league emerged in 2015–16. This new National Women's Hockey League (NWHL) had teams based only in the United States and promised to pay higher salaries. Fans of women's hockey always hoped the CWHL and NWHL would join forces to become one strong league, but instead, the CWHL announced it was folding after the 2018–19 season. Hopes going forward are that the NHL will get involved to help women's hockey grow stronger.

Trophy Tales

Jayna Hefford began playing on Canada's National Women's Team in 1996–97. By the time she retired in 2015, she had won four Olympic gold medals and one silver, as well as seven golds and five silvers at twelve Women's World Championships. Hefford is considered to be the second-greatest player in Team Canada's history — after Hayley Wickenheiser — with 267 games played, 157 goals and 291 points. In 2018, Hefford became the fifth women's player to be inducted into the Hockey Hall of Fame, joining Angela James (Canada, 2010), Cammi Granato (United States, 2010), Geraldine Heaney (Canada, 2013) and Danielle Goyette (Canada, 2017).

When Hefford retired from the Canadian Women's Hockey League in 2013, she was their all-time leading scorer. In 2016, the league named its trophy for Most Valuable Player after her.

Super Sisters

Sisters Marissa and Hannah Brandt have both played Olympic hockey — but for different countries! Back in 1993, the Brandt family was weeks away from completing Marissa's adoption from South Korea when Mrs. Brandt discovered she was pregnant with Hannah. The sisters grew up in Minnesota, doing just about everything together: dance, gymnastics, soccer — and hockey. In 2018, Hannah represented the United States at the PyeongChang Winter Olympics while Marissa represented Korea.

Olympian sisters, Hannah Brandt (right) for Team USA and Marissa Brandt (left) for Team Korea.

MASCOT MAYHEM

Hunter is the lynx mascot of the Edmonton Oilers. He's named after "Wild" Bill Hunter, who was the original Oilers owner. The team started in 1972 as part of the WHA, which is why Hunter wears number 72. Hunter is said to enjoy high-fives and hugs from fans brave enough to approach him.

NAME GAME:
Modern Edition

These days, player nicknames are most likely to be a short form of the player's name. For example, Auston Matthews's Toronto teammates usually call him "Matts" or "Matty." Patrick Marleau is "Patty." Morgan Rielly is "Mo." Maple Leafs coach Mike Babcock is "Babs." Still, not all nicknames are as simple as that. Nazem Kadri is sometimes called "Naz" but he's also "Dreamer." That comes from "Nazem the Dream," which started early in Kadri's Leafs career when people mispronounced his first name as "Na-zeem" instead of "Na-zim." Mitch Marner is often called "Mitchy" or "Marns," but sometimes his teammates call him "Mouse" — short for "Mighty Mouse" —because Marner is on the smaller side for an NHL star.

Trophy Tales

The National Women's Hockey League (NWHL) is a professional league that started in 2015 with four teams based in the United States. The NWHL's championship trophy is the Isobel Cup. It's named after Lord Stanley's daughter. At the time, Isobel Stanley was one of the best women's hockey players in Canada.

An inscription on the front of the trophy reads: "The Lady Isobel Gathorne-Hardy Cup 1875–1963." A further note says: "This Cup shall be awarded annually to the greatest professional women's hockey team in North America. All who pursue this Cup, pursue a dream; a dream born with Isobel, that shall never die." The Isobel Cup was first presented after the NWHL's inaugural 2015–16 season.

NAME GAME:
Classic Edition

Had Mario Lemieux's career not been cut short due to injuries and illness, he might have challenged many of Wayne Gretzky's scoring records. Lemieux had so much skill that he was called "Super Mario," after the legendary video game released in 1985. That's the year Lemieux was an NHL rookie.

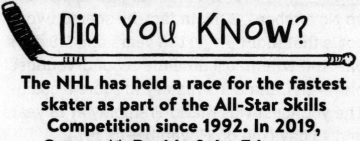

Did You Know?

The NHL has held a race for the fastest skater as part of the All-Star Skills Competition since 1992. In 2019, Connor McDavid of the Edmonton Oilers became the first player ever to win the race three times. His win that year was his third in a row.

Fast Starts in Montreal

Jesperi Kotkaniemi of Finland was chosen third overall by the Montreal Canadiens in the 2018 NHL Entry Draft. He stood out as a star right away but he just seemed to get better and better at Montreal's main training camp. Kotkaniemi wound up making the team and helped the Canadiens get off to a surprisingly good start to the 2018–19 season.

He scored the first goal of his NHL career in a 6–4 win over the Washington Capitals on November 1, 2018. In fact, he scored two goals that night. At just 18 years and 118 days old, Kotkaniemi became the second-youngest player in Canadiens history to score a goal. The youngest was Mario Tremblay at 18 years and 75 days old on November 16, 1974.

Quick Draw!

On November 1, 2018, the Montreal Canadiens set a new NHL record for the fastest two goals, scoring them just two seconds apart! Max Domi scored to put Montreal ahead 5–4 at 19:38 of the third period, and Joel Armia sealed the win with an empty-net goal at 19:40. The Canadiens had rallied from a 4–3 deficit for a 6–4 win over Washington. This exciting game was the same one in which rookie Jesperi Kotkaniemi scored his first two NHL goals.

The previous record for the fastest two goals by one team was three seconds. It was accomplished three times: by the New York Islanders against the Pittsburgh Penguins on November 30, 2016; by the Minnesota Wild against the Chicago Blackhawks on January 21, 2014; and by the St. Louis Eagles against the Detroit Red Wings on March 12, 1935.

NAME GAME:
Team Edition

The QMJHL's original Quebec Remparts
played from 1969 to 1985 and then returned
to Quebec City in 1997. The French word
rempart translates into the English as
rampart, and means the defensive wall
of a castle or city — like the wall that still
surrounds Old Quebec in Quebec City.

All in the Family

Ray Bourque had a stellar 22-year NHL career. He leads all defencemen with 410 goals, 1,169 assists and 1,579 points. Ray won the Norris Trophy as best defenceman five times. It's a tough act for Ray's sons, Chris and Ryan, to follow. They've spent most of their pro careers in the minors, but Chris has equalled Ray one way: he became an Olympic athlete.

Ray Bourque represented Canada at the Nagano Games in 1998, the first time Olympic hockey was wide open to NHL players. When the NHL chose not to let its players take part in the 2018 PyeongChang Olympics, Chris Bourque (who was playing in the AHL) was selected to represent the United States.

The Bourques were just the second father-son duo to play Olympic hockey for two different countries. The first were NHL stars Peter and Paul Stastny. Peter played for Czechoslovakia in 1980 and Slovakia in 2004, before and after his NHL career. Paul played for the United States in 2010 and 2014.

Oh Brother . . .

Over the years in the NHL, four different sets of three brothers have played on the same team at the same time.

Max and Doug Bentley are both in the Hockey Hall of Fame, while Reg Bentley played only 11 games in the NHL. Still, the three brothers played with the Chicago Black Hawks during the 1942–43 season. They even played on the same line, with Max and Doug getting assists on Reg's one and only NHL goal.

Between 1968 and 1972, the Plager brothers played with the St. Louis Blues. Barclay, Bob and Bill Plager were all defencemen.

Stastny brothers Peter, Anton and Marian starred with the Quebec Nordiques in the early 1980s and often played on the same line. Only Peter would make it to the Hockey Hall of Fame.

Through the 2018–19 season, three Staal brothers — Eric, Jordan and Marc — were still active in the NHL. Youngest brother

Jared lasted just two games in the league, but when he made his debut, with the Carolina Hurricanes on April 25, 2013, he played on the same line as Eric and Jordan. Their opponents that night were the New York Rangers. Unfortunately, Marc was injured at the time or else all four Staal brothers could have seen action in the same game.

Did You Know?

Sisters Monika, Nina and Isabel Waidacher played together for Switzerland's National Women's Team at the 2018 Winter Olympics. The three forwards were already teammates with the ZSC Lions women's team in Zurich and had also played together in a few Women's World Championships.

Thanks, Mom

The Ottawa Senators took Brady Tkachuk
fourth overall in the 2018 NHL Entry Draft.
Tkachuk made his NHL debut on October 8,
2018, and in his second game, two nights later,
he scored his first NHL goal. In fact, he scored
two. His mom's birthday was the following
night. "I don't have a gift for her yet," said
Tkachuk. "Maybe I'll try to send flowers, but
this is kind of my gift
for her."

Tkachuk's quick
start also earned
him family bragging
rights. His brother,
Matthew, scored his first
NHL goal, for the Calgary
Flames, in his fourth
career game in 2016–17.
Their father, Keith
Tkachuk, scored his first
goal in his fifth career
game back in 1991–92.

BY THE NUMBERS

Justin Holl played his first NHL game, for the Toronto Maple Leafs, on January 31, 2018, and scored a goal in their 5-0 win over the New York Islanders. The following night, Holl scored again in a 4-0 win over the New York Rangers. Holl was just the sixth defenceman in NHL history to score a goal in each of his first two games. The others were:

PLAYER	TEAM	SEASON
Sprague Cleghorn	Ottawa Senators	1918–19
Rick Lanz	Vancouver Canucks	1980–81
Marcus Ragnarsson	San Jose Sharks	1995–96
Taylor Fedun	Edmonton Oilers	2013–14
Alex Grant	Anaheim Ducks	2013–14

Hockey Player Goes "Boom Boom"

Though it's sometimes said that Bernie Geoffrion invented the slapshot in the 1950s, it might not actually be the case. But it is true that back then coaches didn't like their players slapping the puck. They thought players didn't have enough control over where the puck went. Geoffrion's skill with the slapshot helped to change people's minds. He was nicknamed "Boom Boom" Geoffrion for the *boom* of his stick hitting the puck, followed by the *boom* of the puck striking the boards if it whistled wide of the net.

Boom Boom was one of the biggest stars in hockey when he played with the Montreal Canadiens in the 1950s and 60s. He won the Calder Memorial Trophy as NHL Rookie of the Year in 1951–52 and the Art Ross Trophy as NHL scoring leader for the first time in 1954–55. Geoffrion won his second Art Ross in 1960–61, along with the Hart Memorial Trophy as NHL MVP. Boom Boom had exploded for 50 goals that season to match his childhood idol, Rocket Richard, and become just the second player in league history to hit the 50-goal milestone. Geoffrion was a great team player too. He helped the Canadiens win the Stanley Cup six times in the 14 years he played for them, between 1950 and 1964.

NAME GAME:
Team Names

The Regina Pats of the WHL trace their roots back to 1917. They are the oldest major junior hockey franchise in the world to have continuously operated in the same city with the same name. Originally, the team was called the Regina Patricia Hockey Club, after Princess Patricia, the granddaughter of Queen Victoria. The team's name was shortened to the Pats in 1923.

Lightning Strikes . . . Out

The Tampa Bay Lightning tied the NHL record for wins in a season when they went 62–16–4 in 2018–19. However, things didn't go so well for the Lightning after that. Tampa Bay was swept by the Columbus Blue Jackets in the first round of the playoffs, marking the first time since the 1937–38 season that the first-place team was eliminated from the playoffs without winning even one game.

MASCOT MAYHEM

Spartacat is the mascot of the Ottawa Senators. He is a lion who is known to be quite the acrobat. Spartacat — also known as Sparty — has been Ottawa's mascot since the modern Senators played their first game, on October 8, 1992.

Marvellous Marlies

The Toronto Marlborough Athletic Club was established in the late 1880s. It operated teams in several different sports, including a hockey team that first played in the winter of 1899–1900. Teams known as the Toronto Marlboros played at the highest levels of junior hockey in Ontario from 1902 until 1989.

During those years, the Marlboros won the Memorial Cup as Canadian junior champions a record seven times. Their first title came in 1929 and their last in 1975. A Toronto Marlboros team also won the Allan Cup as senior amateur champions of Canada in 1950.

Since 1931, the Marlboros have had minor hockey teams for boys as well. Many future NHL stars — including Connor McDavid and John Tavares — played minor hockey with them.

The various Marlboros teams were often known as the Marlies. Today, the Maple Leafs' farm club in the AHL is called the Toronto Marlies as a tribute to the long history of the Marlboros.

NAME GAME:
Classic Edition

Dominik Hasek didn't play goal like anyone else. He practically lay down on the ice, flipping and flopping like a fish out of water. Though it didn't always look like it, Hasek knew exactly what he was doing . . . and he would do anything to stop the puck! Hasek's 1.95 goals-against average in 1993–94 made him the first goalie in 20 years to allow fewer than two goals per game, and he led the league in save percentage for six straight seasons. He also won the Vezina Trophy for best goalie six times. Hasek was so good people called him "the Dominator."

Trophy Tales

The Memorial Cup has honoured the junior hockey champions of Canada for more than 100 years. The trophy was donated by the Ontario Hockey Association (OHA) in March of 1919. It was the idea of the OHA's then-president, Captain James T. Sutherland, who had served Canada in World War I. He suggested a trophy to honour the young Canadian hockey players who had given their lives in battle.

From 1919 to 1971, there was a long series of league, provincial and regional playoffs leading to an east-west Final. Since 1972, the Memorial Cup has featured a round-robin playoff involving the champions from each of the major junior hockey leagues: the OHL, the QMJHL and the WHL. Since 1983, the top team from the tournament's host city also gets to play. If the host team happens to have won their league's championship, the team they defeated gets the fourth spot.

MASCOT MAYHEM

Carlton the Bear is the mascot of the Toronto Maple Leafs. He is a 1.93 metre (6 ft., 4 in.) polar bear. Carlton's name and the number 60 he wears on his sweater are tributes to Maple Leaf Gardens, which stood at 60 Carlton Street and was Toronto's home arena from 1931 to 1999. Carlton made his debut on October 10, 1995, at the Leafs' home opener against the New York Islanders.

Did You Know?

Maple Leaf Gardens still stands in downtown Toronto. It's the home of an athletic centre belonging to the city's Ryerson University and still features a hockey rink. But the site is also home to a large grocery store. That means hockey fans who shop there can literally put a biscuit in the basket! (That's a slang term for putting the puck in the net.)

BY THE NUMBERS

On March 12, 2018, Alex Ovechkin scored the 600th goal of his NHL career, in his 990th game. Only three other players in NHL history have reached that milestone quicker than Ovechkin, and only two players did it at a younger age.

PLAYER	GAMES TO REACH 600 GOALS	DATE	AGE
Wayne Gretzky	718	November 23, 1988	27 years, 302 days
Mario Lemieux	719	February 4, 1997	31 years, 122 days
Brett Hull	900	December 31, 1999	35 years, 144 days
Alex Ovechkin	990	March 12, 2018	32 years, 176 days

The Great Eight

The summer of 2018 was certainly a good one for Washington Capitals superstar Alex Ovechkin. He was seen celebrating with the Stanley Cup everywhere: at parades, in a fountain, at the ballpark for a Washington Nationals baseball game, and at soccer's World Cup in his hometown of Moscow, in Russia.

Ovechkin also got to celebrate the birth of his first child, a son named Sergei Aleksandrovich. Sergei was the name of Ovechkin's brother, who died when Alex was only 10 years old. Ovechkin's son was born on August 18, 2018 — 08/18/18 — which was a rather fitting date for the child of a player who wears number 8.

NAME GAME:
Modern Edition

Alex Ovechkin is usually known simply as
"Ovi." But he's also known as "the Great
Eight," and "Alexander the Great," like the
legendary ancient king of Macedonia.

On Target

U.S. women's hockey star Brianna Decker was selected to demonstrate the timed Premier Passer challenge at the 2019 NHL All-Star Skills Competition, and she did more than show them how it was done — she likely had the best time! In this event, players need to perform a series of tricky challenges: connecting with cut-out players; saucering the puck over blocks and into tiny nets; and hitting targets when they light up.

Brianna Decker of the U.S. Women's Hockey team in action at the NHL All-Stars Skills Competition on January 25, 2019.

The challenge is known to rattle even the best players . . . but it was no problem for Decker, who breezed through the demonstration. Fans and viewers clocked her unofficial time at 1:06. This was three seconds faster than the winner of the event, Leon Draisaitl of the Edmonton Oilers, who received the prize of $25,000. Officially the NHL gave her time as 1:12–1:13, but in any case she emerged a winner. The event sponsor decided to also award Decker $25,000 in honour of her super-speedy skills.

 ## Did You Know?

The NHL held its first official Skills Competition back in 1990, on the night before the annual All-Star Game. The NHL uses the contest to showcase the many talents of its star players. The NHL may have gotten the idea from the NBA, which had begun holding a slam dunk contest to show off its stars at its All-Star weekend in 1984.

Full Speed Ahead

In 2019, for the first time ever, a women's hockey player competed in the All-Star Skills Competition. Kendall Coyne Schofield was a member of the U.S. Women's National Team that beat Canada for the gold at the 2018 PyeongChang Winter Olympics. Schofield got a chance to compete in the Fastest Skater contest after Colorado Avalanche center Nathan MacKinnon had to withdraw because of an injury. Connor McDavid won the timed lap event with a result of 13.378 seconds, but Schofield was less than a second off his pace, with a lap of 14.346 seconds. She flew down the ice fast enough for seventh place among the eight competitors, ahead of Clayton Keller of the Arizona Coyotes.

Historic Rivalry?

There are very few rivalries in hockey today that are as intense as the battles between Canada's Women's National Team and the American Women's National Team. Julie Chu is the former captain of the U.S. team, while Caroline Ouellette was Canada's captain at the 2014 Winter Olympics. Ouellette and the Canadian team beat Chu and the Americans to win gold medals at the Winter Olympics in 2002, 2010 and 2014, but Chu's American team beat Canada to win the Women's World Championship in 2005, 2008, 2009, 2011 and 2013.

During the winter of 2010–11, Ouellette and Chu became teammates with the Montreal Stars of the Canadian Women's Hockey League. (The team was later known as Les Canadiennes de Montreal.) While playing together, their icy rivalry melted, and the two fell in love and got married.

Trophy Tales

Stanley Cup wins for each NHL franchise in the Western Conference, Central Division:

Chicago Blackhawks
First season: 1926–27
Stanley Cup wins: 6
Years: 1933–34; 1937–38; 1960–61; 2009–10; 2012–13; 2014–15

Colorado Avalanche
First season: 1979–80
  (Quebec Nordiques through 1994–95)
Stanley Cup wins: 2
Years: 1995–96; 2000–01

Dallas Stars
First season: 1967–68
  (Minnesota North Stars through 1992–93)
Stanley Cup wins: 1
Year: 1998–99

Minnesota Wild
First season: 2000–01
Stanley Cup wins: 0

Nashville Predators
First season: 1998–99
Stanley Cup wins: 0

St. Louis Blues
First season: 1967–68
Stanley Cup wins: 1
Year: 2018-19

Winnipeg Jets
First season: 1999–2000
  (Atlanta Thrashers through 2010–11)
Stanley Cup wins: 0

Lucky Number 7

King Clancy is a Hall of Famer with an NHL career spanning 60 years. Clancy began as a defenceman for the original Ottawa Senators in 1921. He won the Stanley Cup with Ottawa in 1923 and 1927 before being traded to Toronto in 1930 and winning the Cup again with the Maple Leafs in 1932. After retiring as a player, Clancy was an NHL referee before becoming a coach and later a front-office executive in Toronto. Clancy was closely associated with the Maple Leafs until his death in 1986.

Stacey wears number 7, which is the same number that King Clancy wore in Toronto. The Leafs retired number 7 in his honour in 2016.

Laura Stacey, his great-granddaughter, started playing hockey when she was four and went on to become a star player at Dartmouth College in the United States. Stacey first represented Canada on the international stage with the National Under-18 Women's Team in 2010. She appeared in the Women's World Championship for the first time in 2017 and played at the Olympics in 2018. Her great-uncle Terry Clancy, King's son, played hockey for Canada at the 1964 Olympics.

Did You Know?

Tim Horton also wore number 7 during his days with the Toronto Maple Leafs. Though he's better known today for the restaurant chain that he started, Horton is a Hall of Famer who played in the NHL from 1949 to 1974.

Pumpkin Battles

People refer to games between the Calgary Flames and Edmonton Oilers as the "Battle of Alberta." In October of 2018, the rivalry got downright scary when professional pumpkin carver Robbie Beniuk created a Halloween battle between Calgary and Edmonton to support the Little Warriors charity.

Robbie came across an 885-kilogram (1,884 lb.) pumpkin at a fall fair in Smoky Lake, Alberta. He challenged the two cities: whichever donated more money to Little Warriors would win and get its team's logo carved on the ginormous gourd, crushing the loser's logo with its giant, gnarly teeth.

Donations from Edmonton were nearly three times more than from Calgary. The result? A monster Oilers jack-o'-lantern making a meal of the Flames.

NAME GAME: Modern Edition

Hayley Wickenheiser played in her first IIHF Women's World Hockey Championship for Team Canada in 1994 when she was fifteen years old. She went on to have a 23 year career, in which she earned four Olympic gold medals — and several nicknames. Wickenheiser was often called "Wick" for short, but the name that really stuck was "Chicken" — short for Chickenheiser.

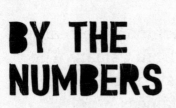
BY THE NUMBERS

On February 16, 2017, Sidney Crosby reached the 1000-point milestone in his NHL career. He did it in his 757th career game, which is the 12th fastest in hockey history. Here are the 11 players who reached the 1000-point mark faster:

PLAYER	GAMES TO 1000-POINT MARK	DATE
Wayne Gretzky	424	December 19, 1984
Mario Lemieux	513	March 24, 1992
Mike Bossy	656	January 24, 1986
Peter Stastny	682	October 19, 1989
Jari Kurri	716	January 2, 1990
Guy Lafleur	720	March 4, 1981
Bryan Trottier	726	January 29, 1985
Denis Savard	727	March 11, 1990
Steve Yzerman	737	February 24, 1993
Marcel Dionne	740	January 7, 1981
Phil Esposito	745	February 15, 1974

10 for 10

The Vancouver Canucks chose Elias Pettersson fifth overall in the 2017 NHL Entry Draft. During the 2017–18 season, he starred for the Vaxjo Lakers in his native Sweden. Pettersson also represented his country at the 2018 World Junior Hockey Championships and the 2018 World Championships, where he played with and against NHL players. Heading into the 2018–19 season, Pettersson was considered the best prospect not yet in the NHL. Even so, his debut with the Canucks that season was better than anyone could have expected. Pettersson scored 10 goals in his first 10 games. That made him just the fifth player in 100 years to score at least 10 goals that quickly. Odie Cleghorn of the 1918–19 Montreal Canadiens scored 12 goals in his first 10 games, while Don Murdoch of the New York Rangers scored 11 in 1976–77. Dmitri Kvartalnov of the Boston Bruins and Rob Gaudreau of the San Jose Sharks each scored 10 in 1992–93.

Did You Know?

The longest game in NHL history featured six overtime periods. Modere "Mud" Bruneteau finally scored at 16:30 of the sixth OT to give the Detroit Red Wings a 1–0 win over the Montreal Maroons on March 24, 1936. That's 116:30 of overtime and 176:30 for the entire game. Newspapers credited Red Wings goalie Normie Smith with making an incredible 90 saves to earn the shutout that night.

Fit to Be Tied

The last tie game in NHL history was a 6–6 draw between the Carolina Hurricanes and the Florida Panthers on April 4, 2004. Brad Fast of the Hurricanes played the only game of his NHL career that night and scored the tying goal at 17:34 of the third period. After a lockout wiped out the entire 2004–05 season, the NHL instituted a shootout rule for games that were still tied after overtime. When the league started up again in 2005–06, games could no longer end in a tie.

Did You Know?

The Bell Centre, home of the Montreal Canadiens, is the largest arena for hockey in the world, with seating for 21,273 fans.

MASCOT MAYHEM

Badaboum was the mascot of the Quebec Nordiques. The Nordiques were an original WHA franchise that began play in 1972 and joined the NHL in 1979. Badaboum was a fuzzy blue seal-like creature who was replaced with Howler the Yeti after the team moved to Denver and became the Colorado Avalanche for the 1995–96 season.

Did You Know?

A Zamboni machine has headlights in case it needs to leave the arena and travel on roads to dump the contents of its snow-collection tank.

NAME GAME:
Modern Edition

Not only is Brent Burns of the San Jose
Sharks one of the best defencemen in the
NHL, he may just have the best nickname
in hockey today. With his scraggly hair
and long, bushy beard, Burns is known as
"the Wookiee" or "Chewbacca," after the
character from the Star Wars movies.

Brent Burns lives up to his nickname during the Breakaway Challenge
at the 2016 All-Star Skills Competition in Nashville, Tennessee.

Trophy Tales

Stanley Cup wins for each NHL franchise in the Western Conference, Pacific Division:

Anaheim Ducks
First season: 1993–94
Stanley Cup wins: 1
Year: 2006–07

Arizona Coyotes
First season: 1979–80
   (Winnipeg Jets through 1995–96)
Stanley Cup wins: 0

Calgary Flames
First season: 1972–73
   (Atlanta Flames through 1979–80)
Stanley Cup wins: 1
Year: 1988–89

Edmonton Oilers
First season: 1979–80
Stanley Cup wins: 5
Years: 1983–84; 1984–85; 1986–87;
 1987–88; 1989–90

Los Angeles Kings
First season: 1967–68
Stanley Cup wins: 2
Years: 2011–12; 2013–14

San Jose Sharks
First season: 1991–92
Stanley Cup wins: 0

Vancouver Canucks
First season: 1970–71
Stanley Cup wins: 0

Vegas Golden Knights
First season: 2017–18
Stanley Cup wins: 0

NAME GAME:
Team Edition

The Hershey Bears are an AHL team from Hershey, Pennsylvania. Hershey chocolate is made in the community, which was built by candy magnate Milton S. Hershey between 1903 and 1905. The Bears have been part of the AHL since the 1938–39 season, which makes them the oldest AHL franchise still playing in their original location.

Milton Hershey established the professional Hershey Hockey Club in 1932. The team became known as the Hershey B'ars — as in chocolate bars. Sportswriters and league officials complained that the name was too commercial, so the Hershey B'ars became the Hershey Bears in 1936. Outside of the "Original Six" teams in the NHL, the Bears are the oldest continuously operating team in professional hockey.

What's in a Name?

The ECHL is a minor professional hockey league two levels below the NHL and one below the AHL. It began play in 1988–89 as the East Coast Hockey League and featured five teams, all based on the east coast of the United States. In 2003, a league known as the West Coast Hockey League folded, and the ECHL took in many of its old teams. Since then, the league has expanded to include teams all across the United States, and currently includes two Canadian teams as well: the Brampton Beast in Ontario and the Newfoundland Growlers. The league is still called the ECHL, but the letters no longer stand for anything!

NAME GAME:
Team Edition

The ECHL has included some of the most unusual team names in hockey history. Currently, their roster includes the Greenville Swamp Rabbits, the Atlanta Gladiators and the Orlando Solar Bears. Over the years, there have been ECHL teams called the Atlantic City Boardwalk Bullies, the Baton Rouge Kingfish, the Chesapeake Icebreakers, the Columbus Cottonmouths, the Jacksonville Lizard Kings, the Louisville RiverFrogs and the Miami Matadors.

The Santa Bears

In 2018, the Orlando Solar Bears of the ECHL wore uniforms that looked like Santa Claus suits for their last home game before Christmas, on December 21. Spectators were encouraged to wear ugly holiday sweaters to the game for a contest. It was also the Solar Bears' annual teddy-bear toss that night, and fans brought teddy bears to throw on the ice after Orlando scored their first goal. The teddies were then collected and donated to local children in need. The Solar Bears were definitely on the "nice" list that night after besting the Florida Everblades 4–3 in overtime.

BY THE NUMBERS

Top five goal-scoring seasons in NHL history:

PLAYER	TEAM	GOALS	SEASON
Wayne Gretzky	Edmonton	92	1981–82
Wayne Gretzky	Edmonton	87	1983–84
Brett Hull	St. Louis	86	1990–91
Mario Lemieux	Pittsburgh	85	1988–89
Phil Esposito	Boston	76	1970–71
Alexander Mogilny	Buffalo	76	1992–93
Teemu Selanne	Winnipeg	76	1992–93

Top five goal-scoring seasons since the year 2000:

PLAYER	TEAM	GOALS	SEASON
Alex Ovechkin	Washington	65	2007–08
Steven Stamkos	Tampa Bay	60	2011–12
Pavel Bure	Florida	59	2000–01
Pavel Bure	Florida	58	1999–2000
Jonathan Cheechoo	San Jose	56	2008–09

Ho-Ho-Hockey

The NHL used to schedule games on Christmas Eve and Christmas Day, beginning in 1919, when, after a late Christmas Eve practice, the Montreal Canadiens caught a morning train to Quebec City to play the Quebec Bulldogs in their one and only season. The Canadiens won that game 12–5. The NHL stopped scheduling games on Christmas Day in 1971 and Christmas Eve in 1972. The NHL also has a roster freeze from 11:59 p.m. on December 19 through 12:01 a.m. on December 28 so that players won't be traded during the holidays.

In Case of Emergency

In the early years of the NHL, teams typically had only one goalie. When that player was injured another player — or even the coach! — had to fill in. But since the 1965-66 season, the league has had a rule that every team has to dress two goalies for every game. If one is injured, a club will bring up a minor-league replacement. But what happens if that goalie can't make it to the arena on time? A team will call in someone from their list of local "emergency" goalies. Only a few of those emergency goalies have ever suited up for an NHL game and none actually played — until New Year's Eve, 2016, in Tampa Bay.

Jorge Alves played hockey in university, and has been working with the Hurricanes' equipment staff since the 2003—04 season. Over the years, Alves would sometimes practise with the Hurricanes and made a few appearances with teams in the ECHL and the Southern Professional Hockey League. On December 31, 2016, the Hurricanes' backup goalie, Eddie Lack, was sick. The team quickly signed Alves to a professional tryout contract so that he could dress as an emergency replacement for that night's game against the Lightning in Tampa Bay. Regular goalie Cam Ward was fine and the Hurricanes were leading 3–1, but with 7.6 seconds left, head coach Bill Peters sent Alves into the game. Alves didn't face a single shot . . . but he could now officially say he played in the NHL.

The stakes were higher for Chicago-area accountant Scott Foster. Foster was born in Canada and played junior B hockey near Sarnia between 1998 and 2002, then played while at Western Michigan University from 2002 to 2006. He later played in a few rec leagues and was one of a crew of goalies the Blackhawks had for emergencies.

Foster had been to 15 games as a backup before, but he didn't suit up until the night of March 29, 2018. Starter Anton Forsberg was hurt before the game against the Winnipeg Jets began. Rookie Collin Delia, just up from the minors, started that night in his first NHL game. But he was injured at 5:59 of the third period. The Blackhawks sent Foster into the net. He took a few warm-up shots, and then it was game on! Foster played the last 14:01 of the game and stopped all seven shots he faced to help Chicago to a 6−2 victory! Foster was later invited to the 2018 NHL Awards show, where he helped present the Vezina Trophy for best goalie to Pekka Rinne of the Nashville Predators.

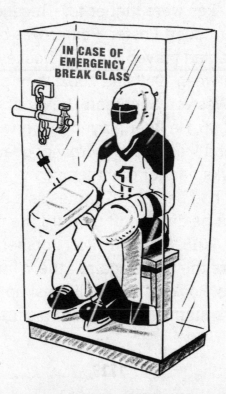

Trophy Tales

It's long been said that the Grey Cup — the championship trophy in Canadian football — was originally intended to be for hockey. According to most stories, Earl Grey, the governor general of Canada from 1904 to 1911, wanted to donate a new amateur hockey championship trophy after the Stanley Cup became the trophy awarded to the champion professional team, starting in 1906. Grey didn't know that the Allan Cup for amateur hockey was already in the works. There were rumours that Grey would donate his new trophy to crown the hockey champions of western Canada instead. But on June 1, 1909, it was announced that Earl Grey's trophy would go to Canada's championship football team — which it still does to this day.

Read even MORE hockey trivia!

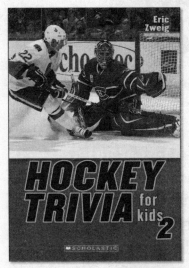

978-0-545-99699-0

978-1-4431-0466-1

978-1-4431-4609-8